Native American Biographies

SITTING BULL

SIOUX LEADER

Elizabeth Schleichert

Enslow Publishers, Inc.

44 Fadem Road	PO Box 38
Box 699	Aldershot
Springfield, NJ 07081	Hants GU12 6BP
USA	UK

Library of Congress Cataloging-in-Publication Data

Schleichert, Elizabeth.
    Sitting Bull: Sioux leader / Elizabeth Schleichert.
        p. cm. — (Native American biographies)
    Includes bibliographical references and index.
    Summary: Examines the life and times of the man who led the Dakota
Indians in their dealings with the U.S. government and in their fight
against the Army troops under General Custer.
    ISBN 0-89490-868-5
    1. Sitting Bull, 1834?–1890—Juvenile literature. 2. Dakota Indians—
Juvenile literature. 3. Hunkpapa Indians—Biography—Juvenile literature.
4. Hunkpapa Indians—Kings and rulers—Juvenile literature. 5. Hunkpapa
Indians—History—Juvenile literature [1. Sitting Bull, 1834?–1890.
2. Hunkpapa Indians—Biography 3. Indians of North America—Great
Plains—Biography. 4. Dakota Indians—History.]
    I.Title II. Series
E99.D1S616 1997
978'.004975'0092
[B]—DC20   96-25592
                                                            CIP
                                                             AC

Printed in the United States of America

10 9 8 7 6 5 4 3 2 1

Photo Credits: Courtesy Little Bighorn National Monument, p. 86;
Jesuit Missouri Province Archives, St. Louis, MO, p. 55; Leo Sutch, p. 19,
27; Little Bighorn Battlefield National Monument, p. 67; National
Archives, p. 6; South Dakota Historical Society, pp. 11, 79; State
Historical Society of North Dakota, pp. 25, 36, 38, 47, 49, 53, 74, 95, 96,
99, 101.

Cover Photo: Denver Public Library, Western History Department

CONTENTS

AUTHOR'S NOTE

Many people mistakenly think that Sitting Bull led the Battle of the Little Bighorn on June 25, 1876, in which Lieutenant Colonel George Custer died. In reality, Sitting Bull acted only as the leading elder and holy man in preparations for the battle. This is just one of the many myths and legends that have grown regarding the greatness of Sitting Bull. This book presents only true facts.

Many myths and legends surround Sitting Bull's life. The facts, however, speak for themselves.

Sitting Bull: Man of Courage and Kindness

When he was a young man, Sitting Bull and a small band of his fellow Hunkpapa Sioux crossed the Yellowstone River to camp on its northern bank. During the night, as they slept, heavy rains hit the ground. The downpour made the river swell and overrun its banks. The following morning, one of the women in the group began weeping and wailing. She had left her favorite horse on the other side of the river where she could see it pawing the ground and neighing.

◈Sitting Bull Steps In◈

There was a flurry of concern and several young men came forward offering to try to retrieve her horse. Sitting Bull said nothing. But slowly he walked about half a mile upstream, where he crossed the river with some difficulty. He then struggled out on the far bank. Approaching the horse, he spoke softly and gently to it, "Grandchild, I have been sent to come to your rescue. Do not run away from me. Somebody is waiting for you on the other side."[1]

After resting a while beside the horse, Sitting Bull again addressed it, "Grandchild, do your best—permit me to guide you across. If you and I reach the other side safely, I shall have the tribe make a dance in your honor."[2]

Then he got on the horse and urged it into the wild river. The raging waters swept them half a mile downstream, but they managed to make it to the other side safely. People rushed to greet Sitting Bull with great cheers and praises. He had shown both courage and kindness. Then everyone began planning the special event that he had promised. It became known as the Sacred Horse Dance.

THE YOUNG
BOY SLOW

In March 1831, winter winds still whistled around the tipis and the snow lay in deep drifts around the Sioux camp. It was during this time that a baby boy was born. At the time of his birth, his people, the Hunkpapa Sioux, were camped on the banks of the Grand River at a place called Many Caches. This place is what we know as northern South Dakota today. According to custom the newborn baby was cleaned with sweetgrass and rubbed down with buffalo fat. Then he was wrapped in robes and laid beside his mother. The boy's parents greeted their first-born son with great joy. The Lakota Sioux cherished their children. They were wonderful gifts from their god, whom they called *Wakantanka*, meaning the Great Mystery.

❖Sitting Bull is Born❖

The baby's father was a proud, highly respected warrior named Sitting Bull.[1] (He would later change his name to Jumping Bull when he gave his son his own name.) He owned many horses. This was a sign of great wealth among his people. The newborn's mother was called Her-Holy-Door. She taught her son a great deal when he was young. All Sioux mothers served as major influences on their sons until they reached adolescence. Then male relatives became the primary influence.

❖Born into the Hunkpapas❖

The tribe into which this newborn boy was born was the Hunkpapas. This tribe was one of seven that formed the larger group known as the Teton or Lakota Sioux. The Lakota Sioux spoke the Lakota dialect and, like other Sioux, were hunters. They lived by following the great herds of buffalo across the Great Plains. Many months were spent moving from one camp to another in search of the buffalo.

The Hunkpapas hunted mainly in the grassy plains west of the Missouri River and north to the mouth of

— ◈ —

This painting by Captain Alfred Sully shows Lakota Sioux at Fort Pierre in 1857. The Lakota or Teton Sioux were the group to which Sitting Bull's Hunkpapas belonged.

the Yellowstone River. The high plains gave way occasionally to wooded plateaus. Buttes, badlands, and small mountains, such as the Black Hills in South Dakota, also broke the miles of gently rolling flat land. A number of rivers flowed eastward into the Missouri River. These rivers formed narrow valleys rich with cottonwood and willow trees.

This was a region of rugged weather, subject to sudden extremes. In the winter, blizzards suddenly blanketed the plains, covering familiar landmarks within hours. In the summer, very little rainfall and a blazing sun posed different challenges. The grass withered to straw and the streambeds dried up. Drought made the search for drinking water and grazing land for horses difficult. Violent thunderstorms would often interrupt the dry spells and cause flash floods and destruction.

❖Living off the Land❖

In this beautiful, but unforgiving, land lived several thousand nomadic members of the Plains tribes, including the Hunkpapas. Whites were rare: only a few trappers and traders, and perhaps an occasional party of explorers ventured into the region. Her-Holy-Door, Sitting Bull, and their people enjoyed all the wealth the land had to offer. Vast herds of buffalo stretching as far as the eye could see supplied most of their wants. There were also deer, pronghorns (an antelope-like animal the size of a large goat with prongs on its horns), elk, and the occasional jackrabbit or bear. Black-tailed prairie dogs, wolves, and coyotes roamed freely while hawks, eagles, and owls soared high overhead. Plains tribes' spirituality was rooted in this landscape and held many of these creatures in respect.

❖Baby Slow❖

Here, the baby born along the Grand River would grow up and learn his people's ways. From the beginning, he showed a distinct personality. He studied everything around him intently and was deliberate in his movements. When given a piece of food, he held it and gazed at it for a time. He did not put it into his mouth right away like most babies. This habit soon earned him the nickname "Hunkesni" or "Slow."

At first, baby Slow was happy in the warmth of his family's tipi. Buffalo-hide walls protected him from snow and rain. Further warmth and security were provided by the warm buffalo robe his mother wrapped him in and the cozy wood-framed cradleboard he was strapped to. His mother propped the cradleboard up against a tipi post to do her chores. In the winter, all of the family's meals were cooked in a pot over an open fire in the center of the tipi. Meanwhile, Slow's father leaned on a backrest in the place of honor opposite the tipi entrance. He rested or talked with friends. Baby Slow spent hours watching his six-year-old sister, Good Feather, playing on the tipi's dirt floor with her dolls and miniature tipis.

In the summer, the sides of the tipi were lifted a few feet off the ground to let cool breezes in. Then, Her-Holy-Door would start the cookfire outside and hang the cradleboard in a nearby tree while she worked and talked with her friends. Slow's father sat nearby, making arrows or mending his weapons. If Slow were upset and started to cry, Her-Holy-Door rushed over and tried to quiet him. Keeping quiet was the first and most important lesson a Sioux baby had to learn. Otherwise, the baby's cries might alert a nearby enemy to the Sioux presence.

Slow's father and the other men were often hunting buffalo, so he spent time as a young child with his mother, his sister, and other relatives. They all helped take care of him and cheered on his efforts to walk. Good Feather especially liked to cuddle and tease him. He was not spanked or harshly scolded. If he were caught doing something wrong, he was gently told to stop.

❖The Sioux Way of Life❖

Slow heard the hunters around the campfire singing their songs in honor of the buffalo. He saw them return from the hunt with their fresh supply of meat, and celebrated with the rest of camp by feasting on roasted buffalo ribs and stews. He watched his mother scraping buffalo hides to make tipi coverings and robes. She would use all of the other parts of the buffalo, too. She made cups and tools from the horns and fashioned the sinews, or tendons, into thread for sewing and strings for the men's bows. She dried strips of buffalo meat in the sun for jerky. This was a food that could last for a long time and did not spoil. She mixed some of this dried meat with fat and berries for another kind of food for long trips, called pemmican. Slow himself participated in the endless ritual of packing up camp, moving, and unpacking again at another campsite, as his family followed the buffalo herds across the plains. His mother took down the family tipi, and loaded all of their things on his father's horses or on a sled, called a travois, which the horses pulled. As a baby, Slow rode in his cradle-board which was hung from a knob—known as a saddle horn—on the front of his mother's saddle. He swung along next to her bundles of herbs, pots, and other things. As Slow got older, he sat behind her on her horse. Then, by the age of eight, Slow rode his own pony when they moved camp.

❖Hunting Trip❖

The first seasonal trip came with the spring. The Hunkpapas broke their winter camp and headed out after the buffalo. Riding as far as twenty-five miles a day, they would await word from the scouts out ahead of them. The scout would find a nearby herd or a suitable campsite. Having reached the site, Slow and the other youngsters helped the women set up the tipis. The men cared for the horses. Slow witnessed the men preparing the prayers, songs, and ceremonies that were performed to ensure a good hunt from the spirits. The men dressed up in buffalo masks and headdresses and pretended to be buffalo with pawing feet. They danced to the sound of drumming and singing. They would often do this for several days without stopping. Then, early one morning, they got up and rode off to the hunt.

Until he was old enough to go off with the men, young Slow and the other Sioux boys spent hours playing hunting games. They sometimes shot each other with miniature bows and arrows. Almost before he could walk, a Sioux boy learned to ride. When he was about seven or eight years old, he started hunting small animals, such as jackrabbits. The importance of becoming a fearless hunter and warrior was taught early. A hunter who brought home meat was to be honored as a provider for many. Slow practiced for hours with his bow and arrows.

❖Childhood Games❖

Slow played other childhood games. Both boys and girls played with animal dolls made in the image of buffalo, bear, and elk. In the winter, children sped down hills on buffalo-rib sleds. Icy ponds and rivers provided a place to play a game called "Throwing It In." Children made five holes in the ice and took turns spinning wooden tops toward one of the holes. They yelled out which hole they were aiming for as the tops spun. In the spring, they played hoop-rolling games and a game in which the children would wrap the end of a short stick with balls of mud and then fling the mud at each other.

Slow began to excel at some of these childhood games. He became the fastest runner in camp, beating the other young boys in all their foot races. By age nine or ten, he continued to play these competitive games well, and he also began to learn skills from his father and his uncle, Four Horns. They would mold him into a hunter and warrior. He had already become skilled with his bow and arrows and showed signs of being an excellent rider. He could guide his pony with the pressure of his knees and legs. Like other boys, he rode bareback, using only a thin piece of rope looped through the pony's lower jaw as a bridle. Four Horns taught him tricks for shooting with a bow and arrow. He also showed him how to make these and other weapons. Slow would someday be able to go with his father and the other men to hunt the buffalo.

Finally, at age ten, Slow's chance came. We do not have all the details from that day, but we can picture it, based on our knowledge of how the Sioux hunted.

◈Slow's First Hunt◈

On that day of his first buffalo kill, Slow was up at sunrise with the rest of the camp. He mounted his pony and rode close to the other hunters. He was careful to keep downwind from the buffalo, so they would not catch his scent and run off. He waited for a sign from the hunt's leaders before heading into the herd. At just that moment, he sighted a young, weak buffalo as his target. He bent low over his pony's neck and quietly urged him on. He silently approached his prey, edging up to it from the right, while grasping his bow in his left hand. Riding up to within firing range, he shot his arrow. It entered the lung, just under the animal's last rib, for a clean kill. After his success, he thanked the buffalo and left a piece of its meat behind as an offering to *Wakantanka,* the god of the Sioux. He might have also left the skull behind, facing the rising sun. This was to try to ensure a good buffalo hunt in the future.

Later, when he returned to camp after his first successful hunt, his father boasted about his son's feat. The other men joined in, showering praise upon him. A boy's first hunt was a milestone in his life. It was a sign that he was maturing into a man. There were reasons for this. Buffalo hunting was extremely dangerous. An angry buffalo might charge a horse and rider headlong. Or a horse might fall in a prairie-dog hole, throwing its rider, who might be crushed or trampled to death. During each hunt, a number of

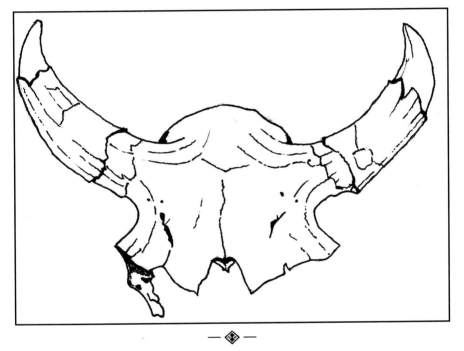

— ◈ —

Sitting Bull kept the sacred buffalo skull with him as he fled north from pursuing troops in 1876. He used it in ceremonies to call upon the animal's protective spirit.

men were either killed or died later from their injuries. Slow not only survived his first hunt, he killed a calf or two. He excelled at it, and went on to many more successful hunts. He always showed exceptional skill and bravery. His people began to notice him, and to expect great things from him. He was soon able to sing with the best of the hunters the Sioux song:

> *I go to kill the buffalo*
> *The Great Spirit sent the buffalo*
> *On hills, in plains and woods.*
> *So give me my bow; give me my bow;*
> *I go to kill the buffalo.*[2]

YOUNG WARRIOR

Slow won prestige for killing his first buffalo at a young age. Now, he set out to prove his skill in another honored Sioux role—warrior. Sioux warriors often fought with Crows, Pawnees, and other enemy tribes. Their aim was to prove their own bravery and courage. Sometimes they would even take a few horses from the enemy. The best way for a man to prove his skill as a warrior was in hand-to-hand combat or simply by charging in and touching an enemy. This was sometimes done with a long stick adorned with a feather at one end. It was called a coup stick. A Sioux would ride up to an enemy warrior, and, at risk of being killed, come close enough to touch him with the stick. This practice was known as "counting coup." It was a sign of great daring or courage.

❖Skilled Horseman❖

Slow spent hours on horseback, shooting his bow and arrows, perfecting his skills. Already, as a young boy, his courage seemed remarkable. One day a Crow, enemy of the Hunkpapas, was killed when he was prowling around Slow's camp. His body was brought into one of the tipis and the boys in camp were told they should touch it. This would prove their courage in the face of death. Slow was the first to do this. He went without hesitation to the dead warrior. He eagerly looked forward to the day when he could go with the men and prove his worth with the best of the warriors.

❖Becoming a Warrior❖

This opportunity came in the summer of 1845, when Slow was fourteen. His people were camped on Powder River (in present-day Montana). A war party of about twenty men, including Slow's father, went out riding in pairs. They were looking for a group of Crows they had heard was in the area. Slow decided to go, too. He painted himself from head to foot, and covered his pony with red paint. He put on a pair of soft leather shoes, a breechcloth, a few strands of beads, and rode out after the men. When he caught up with them, Slow slipped off his horse, put his arm around its neck, and announced to the stunned group, "We are going, too."[1] His father agreed, urging him to try to do something brave, and handed him a coup stick. On the third day out, the party crossed a divide and spotted a party of Crows in a creek below. They charged toward the Crows, who turned and started to flee. Slow was out in front as the Sioux approached. He charged toward a Crow warrior who was about to shoot some arrows. He slapped the warrior on the arm with his coup stick and spoiled his aim. Soon, the Crow left and young Slow won his first honor in battle.

◈Sitting Bull Gets His Name◈

Back at the camp, the war party charged into the tipis announcing what had happened. Slow's father painted his own horse black, the color of victory and honor. He placed Slow on top of the horse. Then, he paraded his son around the camp, shouting, "My son has struck the enemy. He is brave."[2] The next evening, Slow's father gave a feast for him. Slow, painted all over in black, acted out the story of his first coup. The other warriors shouted out their approval. Slow's father announced that from then on, his son would be called *Tatanka-Iyotanka*, or Sitting Bull. This name stood for a buffalo bull under siege who sits back on his haunches and fights until death. He gave his son a white feather to put in his hair as proof of his first coup. He also gave his son a shield with four eagle feathers. The feathers represented courage in each of the four cardinal directions—north, south, east, and west. Hereafter, Sitting Bull would carry the shield as a prized possession and symbol of power. At a young age, this warrior had leapt into the spotlight by demonstrating his bravery in battle. To the Sioux, he had proven his worth and much was expected of him.

◈Wounded in Battle◈

It was not long after this that Sitting Bull added another feather, a red one, to his hair. This was proof that he had been wounded in battle. It happened when he and his people were camped on the Musselshell River north of the Yellowstone. Some Sioux scouts reported that there were unknown parties in the hills around the camp. About fifteen warriors, including Sitting Bull, rode out to investigate these reports. Suddenly, as they rode into a valley, about twenty Flatheads charged them. The enemy dismounted and formed a line behind their horses. They began firing at the Sioux. Sitting Bull rode down the length of the line as arrows and bullets whizzed by him. He was hit just once in the foot. Both sides suffered numerous losses, but the Sioux considered it

— ◈ —

Sitting Bull is depicted in a drawing by No Two Horns (or Joseph has No Two Horns) during the incident when his foot was wounded by a Flathead warrior.

their victory. In the end, the Flatheads rode off to the north, while the Sioux returned to their camp.

In battle after battle, the Hunkpapas and other Teton Sioux pushed their way westward. By the early 1800s, they claimed much of Wyoming, Nebraska, and North and South Dakota as their own. They were fighters who proved themselves a proud force on the Plains.

❖Warrior and Hunter❖

By about 1850, Sitting Bull had achieved the full status or rank of warrior and hunter among his people. Whatever he did, he sought to excel, to do it as well as possible. When he rode out to hunt, he presented a startling sight. He rode naked except for his breech-cloth. His hair was tied behind his ears, and red paint was splashed on his legs, arms, and back, and on his horse's legs. Not many others painted themselves so elaborately for the hunt. Whether in a contest or in a hunt, he was always out in front of the rest. He loved racing and riding fast horses. His fastest horse was a sorrel, a light brown or chestnut horse. The horse's name was Bloated Jaw or Lump on the Jaw. It always got him where he was going ahead of the others.

Sitting Bull's name became feared among Sioux opponents. Sometimes, in his absence, a group of warriors would come across an enemy and one

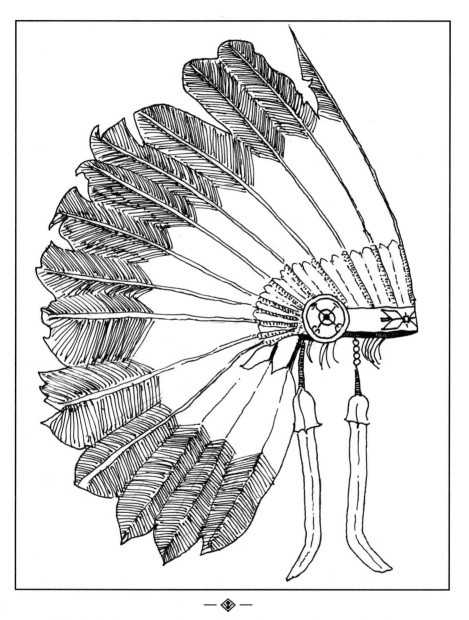

— ◆ —

A typical Sioux war bonnet has two ermine pendants, a beaded brim, and thirty-two eagle feathers in its crown—each representing a deed of valor. A replica is shown here.

would yell out that he was Sitting Bull. This would strike cold fear in their opponents' hearts, often causing them to flee.

During the 1850s, Sitting Bull participated in more than a dozen battles against the Crow and the Assiniboine. He was victorious in each of them. He and the others, returning from a battle, danced, sang, and told stories of their great deeds for several nights. Still, these battles could take a toll on even the best warriors. Once, when he was twenty-five, Sitting Bull was battling a Crow chief. The chief fired a gunshot from a large firearm. It hit Sitting Bull in the foot. That night, he was unable to dance in the victory dance. From then on he always walked with a limp. A few years later, Sitting Bull witnessed his father's death in hand-to-hand combat with a Crow. Sitting Bull continued to win honor for himself. He helped to found an elite warrior society called the Midnight Strong Heart Society. It was named for the late-night ceremonies and feasts it held. Sitting Bull also belonged to several other warrior societies. They all honored and celebrated their members' bravery and courage. But Sitting Bull's reputation was far superior to those of other warriors. He was elected war chief in 1857, at the astoundingly young age of twenty-six.[3] He went on to become chief of the Hunkpapa within the next decade.

MAN OF VISION AND HEART

The Teton Sioux lived close to nature and saw themselves as one with the natural world. They were a spiritual people who believed that everything had a life and a spirit—including all animals, trees, plants, and even the rocks and the streams. The greatest spirit of all was *Wakantanka*, the Great Mystery. According to the Sioux, he could speak to people through snow, wind, trees, water, rocks, eagles, hawks, deer, or buffalo. The Sioux prayed and sang to the spirits and asked for power through these beings. In addition, they believed that certain members of the tribe had special powers to dream or tell the future. These men were called holy men, or *Wichasha Wakan*.

◈Holy Spirits◈

Sitting Bull claimed that *Wakantanka* had begun teaching him special things to lead his people while he was still in his mother's womb. He felt he was destined to be a holy man and to care for his tribe. Events seemed to prove him right. When he was still young, he had an experience that appeared to reveal his powers as a *Wichasha Wakan*.[1]

It happened one summer day after he had been hunting in the woods near the Grand River. He was tired and lay down to rest. Just as he was falling asleep, he noticed a woodpecker peering down at him from a nearby tree. While he dozed, he dreamed a grizzly bear was coming toward him, and he became afraid.[2] The grizzly was feared by most Native Americans. If it attacked a person, its tough hide and thick fur made it difficult to kill. In such a contest, the bear usually won. Sitting Bull's dream was so scary that he woke up and lay there, half awake. Suddenly, he heard the woodpecker pecking twice against the tree trunk. He interpreted this as a warning for him to lie still. A few minutes later, a huge grizzly was, in reality, towering over him. He realized his dream had come true. He followed the bird's advice and did not move. The bear breathed in his face and brushed up against him. A grizzly, however, will rarely harm someone who pretends to be dead. So, it soon took off, leaving Sitting Bull alone. He stood up and saw the woodpecker still there gazing back at him. He reached out his arms as if to bless the bird. Then he made up a song that he sang to the woodpecker.

❖Vision and Prophecy❖

This incident told of Sitting Bull's gift of prophecy and communication with other spirits. It also bonded him forever with the birds. From then on, he learned the ways of the birds and imitated their songs. He claimed that he could understand them. The magpie and the meadowlark, especially, had many times saved his life by warning him of danger. Since birds were such good singers, Sitting Bull also learned to compose and sing. The Sioux had always valued songs, so Sitting Bull's love of song made him popular at tribal gatherings. Often he sang for spiritual purposes and to show his love for his family or for the children of the tribe. He was particularly fond of young people and treated them with kindness.

❖Understanding the Animals❖

Sitting Bull's close bonds to the animal world went beyond a love of birds. His kindness extended to other creatures, too. When he was fifteen, he was again hunting in the woods. He came upon a wolf that had been wounded by two arrows. The story goes that the wolf pleaded with Sitting Bull for help. The young warrior bent down and pulled out the two arrows. Then he cleaned the wolf's wounds. When he was done, the wolf ran off. Afterward, Sitting Bull made up a song about this experience, which he dedicated to all wolves.

❖A Generous Man❖

Sitting Bull demonstrated a quality that was highly regarded by his people—generosity. After the hunt, he often gave those members who had nothing to eat some of the meat from his buffalo. When on the hunt, after killing a buffalo, he would offer up a prayer and leave the whole carcass behind as an offering to the Great Mystery. He seemed always to have the best interests of his people at heart. He prayed often for their good health and for tribal luck. When members of his band became ill, he tried to help. He was not a medicine man but he learned enough of the healing practices to know which herbs or roots to use for various ailments. He knew the rituals and the chants used by medicine men to get rid of the bad spirits. He also did what he could for husbands and wives who were quarreling. He himself knew something about marriage. He had married his first wife when he was twenty years old and later married many more times. (The Sioux accepted the practice of a man, if he could afford it, having several wives at the same time. This was a custom that Sitting Bull followed.)

❖The Sun Dance❖

But for all his kindness to others, it was his ability to see things through dreams and visions that ultimately set Sitting Bull apart. He felt that to truly call himself a holy man, however, he must sacrifice himself in some significant way to the spirits. In 1856, when he was twenty-five, he participated for the first time in that most important of Sioux ceremonies, the Sun Dance. The Hunkpapas were camped on the east side of the Little Missouri River that June. Their tipis were in a circle, as was the custom. The center was left open for songs, games, and tribal ceremonies. Some of the men went off to gather trees in order to build a Sun Dance lodge. It would be framed with twenty-eight posts with a sacred pole placed in the middle. An altar made of a buffalo skull would be placed here. The pole connected the sky and the earth and the skull symbolized all of life.

Sitting Bull prepared before the Sun Dance. He stripped himself of all garments and entered the small domed structure called a sweat lodge. Once inside, he breathed in the steam made by pouring water over the red-hot stones in the center of the floor. Sitting Bull soaked up the steam through all his pores. It cleansed his mind and body of all that might cause disease, wrong thinking, or exhaustion. After a sweat bath, each man who was to dance approached the Sun Dance Lodge. The dance began when Sitting Bull and the other men started circling the sacred pole. They were attached to it by long ropes tied to small wooden skewers that penetrated the flesh of their chest. Over the next eight days or so they would dance and fast for hours to the music of drums and eagle-bone whistles. They would also look directly at the sun, until they were in a sort of religious trance. As part of their sacrifice, they might gash their arms with knife cuts. Near the end, they would hang in the air, held by the skewers, with the weight of their bodies tearing their own flesh until they were able to pull themselves free. This kind of torture was considered the highest form of spiritual self-sacrifice. It left wounds that marked a man for life. He wore these wounds proudly as proof of his bravery in the face of pain. Sitting Bull, over his lifetime, performed so many Sun Dances that his back and chest were covered with deep scars. In this, his first Sun Dance, he did all that was expected of him. At the height of his suffering, he reached a state of ecstasy where he heard *Wakantanka* telling him that all his prayers for his people's well-being would be answered. As the skewers ripped out pieces of his skin, he felt happy. He knew he had pleased the Great Mystery and been elevated to the rank of holy man.[3]

❖A Holy Man❖

As a newly initiated holy man, Sitting Bull was given a pipe for use in all tribal religious ceremonies. The pipe acted as a sort of moveable altar for offering up the sacrifice of smoke to the spirit world. The Sioux believed that the smoking of the pipe—using a mixture of tobacco and aromatic herbs—opened up communication with *Wakantanka*. Those holding the pipe spoke nothing but the truth. Pipe ceremonies made holy numerous tribal decisions. The Sioux never went to war without a pipe ceremony. They never declared peace without it. This is how the name "peace pipe" came to be. Sioux pipes could reach five feet in length. They were marked by a carved red stone bowl and a wooden stem covered with birdskins and dangling eagle feathers. Participants in a pipe ceremony sat in a circle. Sitting Bull or one of the other select tribesmen lit the pipe. He, as well as the others, in turn, held it up as an offering of smoke to the sky and to the earth. Then they moved it to each of the four compass directions before taking a puff. The pipe was then passed around clockwise, in the direction it was believed the sun traveled. Each participant followed this ritual. Often, he (only men participated in the pipe ceremony) spoke. He prayed, making a personal prayer to *Wakantanka* or offering up a vow to be honored later. Great decisions and special occasions all called for a pipe ceremony. Sometimes, Sitting Bull went on his

— ◈ —

Sitting Bull is pictured with his sacred pipe. It was used to offer up the sacrifice of smoke to the spirit world.

own to a hilltop to seek closer ties with the Great Mystery or offer up his own spiritual vows. Both were done in the form of a solitary pipe ceremony.

❖Natural Leader❖

After his initial Sun Dance, Sitting Bull continued to demonstrate his extraordinary leadership. He seemed to draw people to him. Some indefinable quality made almost everyone like him. He never pretended to be someone he was not. He never acted superior. Few could find fault with him. However, on occasion, his compassion, even toward his enemies, caused others to question his judgment. For instance, in 1857, Sitting Bull was taking part in a battle against some Assiniboine, north of the Missouri River. He was thrown off his horse and landed in a shallow lake. As he got out of the water, he spotted a young Assiniboine boy. The boy was about eleven years old and had been captured by Hunkpapas. The Sioux were prepared to kill the boy. He seemed courageous and showed little fear of death. When he saw Sitting Bull stumbling out of the water, he cried out to him. He called him big brother. Sitting Bull told the others to let the boy go. He claimed the boy was too brave to die. The warriors argued with Sitting Bull. They insisted that they be allowed to deal with their prisoner on their own terms. But Sitting Bull won in the end. He took the boy back to camp with him, and adopted him as his own brother. Perhaps the death of his own

— ❖ —

This drawing by No Two Horns represents the adoption by Sitting Bull of the Assiniboine youth who came to be called Stays Back.

four-year-old son earlier that year (from typhoid fever) had made Sitting Bull soft-hearted. The boy, who came to be called Stays Back, grew up to be a fine warrior. He was loyal to Sitting Bull until Sitting Bull's death.

Soon, however, Sitting Bull would face an enemy so numerous, so powerful, and so determined, that no amount of vision, compassion, wisdom, or bravery could ultimately save him or his people from the impact.

The Greatest Challenge

The challenge Sitting Bull and his people were about to meet came from a new people, the *Wasichus*. This was what the Hunkpapas called white men. When Sitting Bull was a boy, he hardly ever saw any *Wasichus*. He might have seen an occasional trader at Fort Pierre, on the upper Missouri River. The fort was the main trading outlet for the Hunkpapas. Here they exchanged buffalo robes for trade goods, such as guns, ammunition, and metal tools. Most of what Sitting Bull knew of this strange people came from tales he had heard from other tribes.

Most whites never came as far west as Sitting Bull's land. It, along with the rest of the western half of the present-day United States, was considered "Permanent Indian Country." The government believed it was mostly a barren desert, of little value. To them, it was appropriate only for the natives.[1]

❖White Settlers Arrive❖

This situation changed rapidly, however. By 1840 the population of the United States grew to twenty million whites, as compared to about four-thousand Hunkpapas.[2] The white settlements were just five hundred miles to the southeast of Sitting Bull's people, along the outskirts of the prairie. In the East, more and more immigrants from Europe were crowding into New York, Boston, and Philadelphia. They were pushing the boundaries of these cities out into the surrounding regions. Before long, inexpensive, available land in the East was gone. Many people began to look to the West as a land of opportunity. In the 1840s they began streaming toward the fertile valleys in Oregon. They came over the Plains in covered wagons, following a route to the south of Sitting Bull and his people. But they kept coming. In 1846 the entire Oregon Territory became part of the United States. Two years later, California and the entire Southwest became part of the country. This came as a result of the treaty ending the war between the United States and Mexico. That same year, gold was discovered in California. It suddenly appeared that the West might not be a barren desert after all. Americans developed a sudden interest in exploring and even settling these new lands.

By the time Sitting Bull had become a chief in the late 1850s, the Hunkpapas were starting to feel the effects of western migration. Fortune seekers were streaming toward newly-discovered mines in California, Oregon, Washington, Idaho, and Montana. A few years later, things would worsen for the Hunkpapas. Rumors of gold near the headwaters of the Missouri, deep in their territory, erupted. The white settlers trampled over the Hunkpapas' hunting grounds. They left behind tin cans, carcasses of dead horses and oxen, and other remnants of their camps along the trail. Game, such as elk and deer, was becoming scarce, too.

Sitting Bull had no quarrel with the whites, as long as they stayed out of his people's territory. Sitting Bull and his people wanted to be left alone to hunt and pursue their traditional livelihood on the Plains. Although this view was at odds with the seemingly unstoppable westward movement, it was not unreasonable. After all, Sitting Bull's ancestors had hunted and traveled this land for a long time. Sitting Bull and his people believed that no one person or persons could claim the land. It came from *Wakantanka,* just as the sea and the sky did. Just as these could not be owned, neither could the land. Most whites failed to understand this viewpoint. Instead, they assumed that the land was theirs for the taking, and that the Native Americans had no right to be there. Many believed that the Native Americans were an inferior people—savages. They should be done away with or placed in a controlled environment on reservations. They should be "civilized" by being forced to abandon their nomadic hunting existence and taught how to settle down and farm. To enforce their viewpoint, the white people brought soldiers into "Indian country" and treated the tribes as outlaws.

◈ Disputes Arise ◈

Among the Hunkpapas and other Sioux, the issue of how to deal with the whites intensified. It continued to cause bitter disputes. Some Sioux engaged in isolated attacks on whites, whom they viewed as trespassers in their territory. Sitting Bull did not consider himself at war with whites. He was deeply troubled, however, by what he heard from other Plains tribes about what whites were doing to them. They told of how the tribes were being forced by white men to give up their hunting way of life. They were being removed onto reservations. Sitting Bull did not want his people to be penned up on a reservation and deprived of the land that they had moved over freely for generations. He was determined to hold fast to his ancestors' sacred grounds and the traditional ways of his people as long as possible.

◈Gold Seekers◈

In 1863 hundreds of gold seekers were streaming into Hunkpapa territory. United States troops also arrived in the Dakotas. Their task was to subdue the Sioux and other Plains tribes by force, if necessary. This would allow the miners and other emigrants to pass through the territory unharmed by hostile bands. So began the warfare between the United States and the Plains tribes. It would last for more than two decades and involve more than two hundred battles. One clash in nearby Minnesota had effects on Sitting Bull's people. There, the Sioux had been pushed onto a reservation where they were not given enough to eat. Close to starvation, some of them attacked and killed several hundred white people. The governor of Minnesota sent in Colonel Henry H. Sibley to fight the Sioux. About the same time, a drought had forced Sitting Bull and the Hunkpapas to venture further east on the far side of the Missouri River to hunt. Here, many Minnesota Sioux who had been battling Colonel Sibley fled to the Hunkpapas for safety. Sitting Bull was determined to help the rest of them escape. He reportedly joined in and clashed with Sibley's forces in late July 1863. According to some accounts of these battles, at one point Sitting Bull charged forward under heavy fire toward Sibley's wagon train and touched a mule driver. Despite fierce resistance by the Sioux, Sibley's forces won.

Sitting Bull had little respect for the white soldiers. He told his tribesmen they "do not know how to fight. They are not lively enough. They stand still and run straight," he said. He noted something else about the soldiers:

> Also, they seem to have no hearts. When an Indian gets killed, the other Indians feel sorry and cry, and sometimes stop fighting. But when a white soldier gets killed, nobody cries, nobody cares.[3]

❖Power of the White Man❖

Sitting Bull spoke the truth about his enemies. They were, in fact, often strangers to one another. Many were immigrants only recently arrived from Ireland, Germany, and other countries. They often joined the army because they had nothing else to do. Often they could not speak English.

The soldiers however had the power of numbers behind them. They also had a determined federal government. It wanted the natives subdued and placed on reservations. Several thousand soldiers soon arrived in the Upper Missouri region to secure it for themselves. They built a new fort a few miles below Fort Pierre, called Fort Sully. In the summer of 1864, they prepared a new attack against the Native Americans. Their orders were to punish those involved for the uprising in Minnesota. It made little difference whether they found the right tribe of Sioux or not. To the United States Army, any Native American was a fair target.

A coalition of various Sioux and Cheyenne tribes came together to try to stop the soldiers. The tribes were camped on the Little Missouri River by a mountain they called Where-They-Killed-the-Deer. When soldiers were spotted marching toward them, they withdrew further up the mountain. They waited for the right moment to attack. The soldiers pursued them and began firing rounds of gunfire. Sitting Bull and the other warriors fought back, but without success. The soldiers advanced. The warriors formed a circle around their campsite to allow the women and children to escape. Soon, they realized they could not hold the soldiers off any longer. They scattered up the mountainside.

Sitting Bull had fought bravely but the army's superior rifles, cannons, and six-shooters had proved to be too much. He and some of the other warriors had hoped to save the tipis and other possessions that they had had to leave behind. The next morning, they rode back down to their deserted camp with a white flag held high, as a gesture of peace. But the soldiers ignored the flag and opened fire. Back in the shelter of the woods, the Sioux watched as the white soldiers set fire to the Sioux camp. Tipis, buffalo robes, and other clothing all went up in smoke. The army then ignited the trees and grass surrounding the camp to complete the destruction.

❖Man of Compassion❖

Sitting Bull witnessed many such acts by white soldiers. He did not, however, hold hate in his heart toward these invaders of his territory. In fact, sometimes, he was capable of great compassion toward his supposed enemy. Once, during a battle with white soldiers, some Oglala Sioux (another Teton Sioux tribe) had taken captive a white woman, named Fanny Kelly. Sitting Bull knew Kelly. She had been traded to a Hunkpapa and brought to his village. He could tell that she was homesick and unhappy. He overruled the wishes of other Hunkpapas. In December 1864, Sitting Bull arranged for a group of Blackfeet Sioux (a Teton Sioux tribe) to escort Kelly to a nearby fort. They delivered her, wrapped in buffalo robes, to the army, four months after she had been taken captive. "She is out of our way," Sitting Bull commented. Noting that she had been longing for her people, he said, "So I sent her back."[4]

❖A Way of Life❖

Sitting Bull showed acts of kindness toward individual white people. However, he held firm in his attitude toward the onslaught of this force, as a whole. He refused to compromise his principles. He remained a leader of that faction of Hunkpapas that was determined never to surrender its way of life. He intended to live on the land as he always had. The white soldiers, however, seemed equally determined.

— ◈ —

Fort Buford was one of several forts built by the Army along the Missouri River deep in the heart of Hunkpapa territory. Buford was built in 1866 across the mouth of the Yellowstone River and was especially hated by the Sioux. Sitting Bull's warriors attacked it soon after it was built and set fire to rows of firewood there.

The United States Army built two more forts on the upper Missouri River deep in the heart of Hunkpapa territory: Fort Buford, opposite the mouth of the Yellowstone; and Fort Stevenson, across from the Little Missouri. To Sitting Bull, these new forts represented the most fearful intrusion yet. He concentrated his people's efforts on hit-and-run raids against the forts. He let the army know it was unwelcome.

Some in his tribe were willing to make peace with the whites and accept gifts from them. Sitting Bull refused. He realized that the whites might kill or capture him, but he would hold out as long as he could. He made fun of those who went willingly to reservations, saying "You are fools to make yourselves slaves to a piece of bacon fat, some hardtack [hard biscuits of flour and water], and a little sugar and coffee."[5]

❖Sun Dance❖

Near the end of the 1860s, during the annual Sun Dance celebration in June, several Sioux tribes, as well as some Cheyennes and Arapahos, gathered. They were there to select a chief of all these area tribes. The chief would lead them during these troubled times. Sitting Bull, already a chief of the Hunkpapas, received this honor. The people built a ceremonial lodge for him. Some of the warriors took a buffalo robe and brought it to Sitting Bull in his tipi. He sat down upon the robe, and the warriors carried him back to the new lodge. They all smoked a

— ✦ —

This buffalo robe was tanned by Sitting Bull's wives and painted by him. Buffalo robes were used by the Hunkpapas during ceremonies and were also given as gifts.

ceremonial pipe and pointed it to each of the four winds to ensure that no ill wind would harm them. They prayed to *Wakantanka*. The warriors made speeches. They praised Sitting Bull for his great bravery and courage in battle. They declared their loyalty to him. They vowed they would follow him whatever he commanded them to do—whether it was to make war or press for peace. Then they gave him gifts: a new gun, a bow and arrows, and a war bonnet, adorned with eagle feathers and weasel fur. The warriors took their new chief outside. They lifted him up on a beautiful white horse and led him around the camp in a grand circle.

Sitting Bull sang a new song as he rode on his magnificent horse:

> *Ye tribes, behold me.*
> *The chiefs of old are gone.*
> *Myself, I shall take courage.*[6]

The Black Robe, a Peace Treaty, and the Railroad

Just before Sitting Bull was elevated to his new status, the United States government decided to negotiate a peace treaty with the Hunkpapas and other Sioux tribes. The government wanted to end the wars and remove the threat along the main routes used by settlers heading west. These included an overland wagon trail, the Platte River Road, and two railroad lines—the Union Pacific Railway, and the Kansas Pacific Railway. Two large reservations, one north of

Nebraska and one south of Kansas, were established as a means of confining the tribes in this region.

❖Treaty Signed❖

In 1867 many of the southern Plains tribes signed a treaty with the government. They agreed to move to the southern reservation. Chiefs of two Teton Sioux tribes, Oglala and Miniconjou, whose territory lay south of Sitting Bull's, also agreed to peace terms. In 1868, the government needed Sitting Bull's people to agree, as well.

Officials arranged for a priest, Father Pierre-Jean De Smet, to visit Sitting Bull in the eastern Montana Territory. He was camped there with several hundred followers on the south side of the Yellowstone River. Father De Smet, missionary to the Blackfeet and Flathead tribes, had often traveled among the various tribes. They called him the Black Robe.

As he approached Sitting Bull's encampment, in late June 1868, Father De Smet was impressed by what he saw. Sitting Bull and his warriors presented quite a spectacle. "Plumes of eagle and other birds adorned their long hair," the priest later wrote, and were "mingled with silk ribbons and scalps captured from their enemies. Each one had his face daubed according to his own likes with black, red, yellow, and blue."[1]

Sitting Bull's presence was especially powerful. He was still limping from the Crow bullet he had taken

— ◈ —

Father Pierre-Jean De Smet spent many years among the Native Americans of the West, and served as frequent mediator of disputes between Native Americans and whites. He traveled in 1868 to the Hunkpapa camp to confer with Sitting Bull and his chiefs. He was trying to win their acceptance of the Fort Laramie Treaty.

in his foot years before. His whole being, however, radiated confidence and strength. In contrast Father De Smet had a short, sturdy build and a kind, gentle manner. Sitting Bull ordered one of his men to bring the priest's baggage to his tipi. Sitting Bull gave his guest something to eat and let him rest. Then Sitting Bull spoke his mind to Father De Smet. He noted that the whites had provoked him to attack because of their cruelty to other tribes. He referred specifically to an 1864 army attack on a Cheyenne camp at Sand Creek, Colorado. It had caused the deaths of more than a hundred innocent women and children. Sitting Bull noted that, despite his past attacks on whites, he stood ready to become peaceful toward them, as long as they would withdraw from his territory.

❖Formal Council❖

The next day, Sitting Bull held a formal council with Father De Smet and the Hunkpapa chiefs. Hundreds of tribesmen as well as another ring of older men, women, and children were arranged behind the council lodge. Nearly the entire village was represented. The ceremony began with the lighting of the pipe. Father De Smet puffed and then handed it to the other chiefs. Each took a few puffs, and passed it along. Father De Smet spoke and his words were translated so all could understand his message. He had come, he said, to ask the Sioux to meet with representatives of the Great Father at Fort Rice (in

— ❖ —

This drawing shows Father Pierre-Jean De Smet during one of his many conferences with Native Americans.

southern North Dakota). Sitting Bull welcomed the Black Robe. He agreed to allow some Hunkpapas to go with De Smet to meet with the whites about a treaty. Sitting Bull said that he would agree to whatever was decided upon at that meeting. However, he quickly added that he did not plan to sell any of his land to the whites. He also insisted that the soldiers abandon the forts along the Missouri.

That evening the Sioux enjoyed a friendly gathering with Father De Smet. He blessed many children and told stories of miracles and saints from the Bible. As a token of his esteem for the chief, he gave Sitting Bull a crucifix of brass and wood.

The next day, Sitting Bull rode part of the way with De Smet and his party as they left for Fort Rice. When the party got to the mouth of the Powder River, Sitting Bull gave a short speech. He recalled what they had agreed upon the day before. Then he sent off some of his lesser chiefs, including one named Gall, to speak for him at Fort Rice. Gall had almost been killed by white soldiers a few years before. Sitting Bull knew how much Gall hated the white men. The chief figured Gall would defend the old ways and would stand up to the peace commissioners.

❖No Peace❖

The white commissioners at Fort Rice were not going to negotiate anything. They had decided to simply present the Fort Laramie Treaty, which the Oglala had already signed, to Gall and the other Sioux. The peace commissioners suggested that the Sioux might be happier if they abandoned their hunting way of life and settled down as farmers. In response, Gall spoke:

> *Suppose the people living beyond the great sea should come and tell you that you must stop farming and kill your cattle, and take your houses and lands, what would you do? Would you not fight them?* [2]

He demanded that the whites abandon their military posts along the Missouri and that their steamboats and homesteaders stop coming. Nonetheless, on July 2, 1868, he signed a treaty that addressed none of his grievances. The Fort Laramie Treaty created a "Great Sioux Reservation," located in the western part of what would become South Dakota. Here the Sioux were encouraged to settle down, be fed by the white men's government, be educated, and be taught how to farm. But the treaty also gave the Sioux another piece of land called "unceded Indian territory." It was bounded by the Powder River west of the Bighorn Mountains. It included large chunks of what is now North Dakota, Nebraska, Wyoming, and Montana. This included the Black Hills, which the Sioux held sacred. According to the treaty, "No white person or persons shall be permitted to settle upon or occupy any portion [of the Powder River country]; or without consent of the Indians—to pass through the same." [3] The Sioux secured for themselves their right to hunt in this territory "for as long as buffalo may range."[4] But it also required the Sioux to give up their right to permanently occupy any land off the reservation.

❖Treaty Not Signed❖

Sitting Bull did not sign the treaty. He had not agreed to any of these terms. It was not customary, anyway, for one chief to agree to the terms of a document that another had signed. He and his followers paid little attention to it. About one third of the Teton Sioux population ignored the treaty completely. They moved freely through the territory, as they always had. Others agreed to move onto the reservation, where they received government food. Often, however, these handouts were spoiled and unedible. A few of Sitting Bull's followers drifted on and off the reservation. They visited relatives or spent the winter where a food supply of some sort was available.

For Sitting Bull, the old way of life continued for a number of years. By the mid-1870s, he had two wives and seven children, including two sets of twins. Among the children he had adopted was his sister's son, who was deaf and unable to speak.

Still, things were not really as they once had been. Just two years after the signing of the treaty, thousands of white people passed through or settled on Sitting Bull's lands. In fact, the population of white citizens living west of the Mississippi more than doubled over the next few decades, from seven

million to seventeen million.[5] By 1869 the transconti-
nental railroad was completed across the Plains.

◈Things Get Worse◈

For Sitting Bull, things worsened in the early 1870s. At
this time officials of the Northern Pacific Railroad
determined that they wanted to build a line connect-
ing St. Paul, Minnesota, with Seattle, Washington.
They started sending surveyors to Sioux territory in
the fall of 1871. The rail line intersected the
Yellowstone Valley. This was the heart of the
Hunkpapas' hunting ground. It was also part of the
unceded lands promised the Sioux as their exclusive
domain by the Fort Laramie Treaty. The Yellowstone
River ran through a wide, lush valley filled with cottonwood and willow trees. Here, huge herds of
buffalo and other game roamed. The Hunkpapas had
recently fought for and won this valley from the
Crows. There was no way the Sioux were going to
allow a rail line to ruin their beloved land. A rail line
to the south had already resulted in the killing of tens
of thousands of buffalo. White men rode the railroads
equipped with guns to shoot buffalo, both for sport
and profit. Buffalo hides were sold for a few dollars
each. Then they were shipped back East for leather
goods, robes, and rugs. More than three million of
these animals were slaughtered between 1872 and
1874.[6] (By 1880 the herds were completely destroyed.)

If the railroad came through Hunkpapa territory, it would mean the end of their buffalo, too.

❖The Silent Eaters❖

Sitting Bull met with a small group of his most respected warriors. They had formed a group called the Silent Eaters, dedicated to the welfare of the entire tribe. They held secret midnight gatherings, and dined on the best cuts of buffalo. They discussed what was to be done to solve this problem. Sitting Bull led the group. He urged the warriors to cement their ties with other Plains tribes against the approaching train line. Sitting Bull had already become friends with the Oglala Sioux chief named Crazy Horse. He and Crazy Horse did not want to start a war. War might come, however, and they were determined to be ready.

❖Plans for a Railroad❖

In August 1872, a second railroad surveying expedition arrived. It was accompanied by two groups of soldiers. Sitting Bull and his warriors were encamped not far away on the Powder River. They kept an eye on the surveyors, who were working along the south bank of the Yellowstone River under heavy cavalry escort. A railroad was being planned here. This was a violation of the Fort Laramie Treaty. Sitting Bull's warriors wanted to attack the surveyors, but Sitting Bull restrained them. He hoped to work out a peaceful solution with the whites. But some of the younger, hot-headed braves, eager for a fight, ignored Sitting Bull's wishes. They slipped out in the middle of the night, stole some horses from the surveyors' camp, and triggered a battle with the soldiers. A Sioux warrior was wounded. The fighting went on for several hours. The soldiers hid behind the old creek bank and kept up a continual volley of shells. The white men fought back from the bluffs above the valley. Sitting Bull and Crazy Horse observed the battle from the heights. Sitting Bull saw that the fighting was evenly matched. The soldiers could not be coaxed out into the open, and the warriors could not risk charging their line.

So, Sitting Bull, in a gesture of bravery and lack of respect, staged a spectacle. Just as the early morning sun's rays bathed the valley in brilliant hues of gold, he gathered his pipe and tobacco pouch from his horse. He dismounted and carried his bow, arrow quiver, and rifle with him. He walked down from the bluffs to the open valley. Once out in the meadow between the two forces, he sat down and lit his pipe. He turned and called to the warriors above, inviting whomever wanted to join him to come down. Before long, four other men came forward and sat down with Sitting Bull. They puffed quietly on the pipe, passing it from one to the other. All the time, the soldiers' bullets kept whizzing by them, kicking up balls of dirt and grass. When the tobacco had all been smoked, Sitting Bull grabbed a stick, cleaned out the bowl, and put the pipe back in its pouch. He then turned and walked deliberately back to his tribesmen and told them that they had done enough fighting for one day. They all turned and left. So ended the Battle of Arrow Creek. Sitting Bull's courageous act of defiance was later recounted over and over, adding to his legendary status among his people.

❖Battles Continue❖

There were a number of other battles during the summer of 1872 and the next year between soldiers protecting railway surveyors and the Sioux. But then in 1873, just as quickly as they had come, the surveyors disappeared. Plans for building the Northern Pacific Railroad suddenly died. This had little to do with Sitting Bull's resistance. Instead, it was due to a nationwide economic slump. This meant that Eastern banks could not finance another railroad. It would be six years before the new line was built. By this time much had happened to the Sioux and their allies.

Army and government officials remembered the Hunkpapa resistance against the railroad. No longer was there talk among them of making peace with Sitting Bull and his people. Sitting Bull held back from issuing a call for total war on the whites. He merely wanted to delay and discourage their entry into his people's land. He told his tribesmen that if the soldiers returned and began shooting, then they should shoot back. Surrender was not an option, not now, not ever.

Sitting Bull recalled an experience he had had many years before. As a young warrior, he had been walking in the sacred Black Hills when he heard a man's voice singing a song he had never before heard. He climbed up into the hills, looking for the singer, but he could not find him. Just as he was about to give up, he gazed upward and saw a huge eagle. It was circling overhead. The bird must have been the one singing. The Hunkpapas believe the eagle is closest to the Great Mystery. So, Sitting Bull realized, it must have been *Wakantanka* who was singing to him through the eagle.

And now Sitting Bull found himself singing the same song during these troubled times:

> *My Father has given me this nation*
> *In protecting them I have a hard time.*[7]

THE NOOSE TIGHTENS

Paha Sapa, "Hills That Are Black," was the Sioux name for the dark, forested mountains known as the Black Hills or Badlands of western South Dakota. They rise as high as seven thousand feet above the thick green grass of the plains. These hills had long been sacred to the Sioux. The mountains provided pine poles for tipis, a ready supply of deer and other game for meat, and sheltered sites for winter encampments. These hills had been part of the territory set aside for the Sioux by the Fort

Laramie Treaty. For years the region had remained largely unknown to whites. However, in the 1870s, people in the East began to speculate about the possibility of gold here.

❖Gold in the Black Hills❖

In July 1874, Lieutenant Colonel George Armstrong Custer led a force of more than one thousand soldiers and civilians into the Black Hills to investigate this rumor. Several geologists had come along to look into the gold question. Before long, a nugget of gold had been discovered on the side of a high hill that the Sioux called Mountain Goat. It was a tiny nugget, not worth more than a dime, but Custer and the press turned it into headlines. Custer, known as Long Hair by the Native Americans for his long golden locks, sought personal glory. He was only thirty-five years old, but he was already famous throughout the country as a Civil War hero. He was regarded by an adoring public as a dashing, fearless figure. Those who saw him up close in action were less impressed. They thought he endangered his own soldiers with his risky fighting tactics. With the news coming from Custer's expedition of an actual gold finding, it did not take long before there was talk of ore on every slope. It was rumored that there was enough gold to make anyone who went to the Black Hills rich. *Paha Sapa*, it seemed, would no longer be set aside as sacred ground for the Sioux.[1]

— ❖ —

This portrait shows George Armstrong Custer, a celebrated Civil War soldier. He rose to the rank of lieutenant colonel and gained a reputation as a fighter against Native Americans.

Word of the gold discovery spread rapidly, and prospectors began heading for the Black Hills. Frontier towns, such as Bismarck, Yankton, and Omaha became supply centers for those seeking their fortune. Initially, government troops tried to hold back the gold miners. They wanted to buy the Black Hills from the Sioux in order to make the gold running legal there. Early in 1875, a treaty commission from Washington went to the Sioux. They wanted to see how much the Sioux wanted for the Black Hills. Sitting Bull and others refused to even meet to discuss the sale of any of Sioux lands to the government. For dramatic emphasis, Sitting Bull leaned over and pinched a speck of dirt between his fingers. This indicated that he would not consider the sale of even that much land to the government.

The Sioux living on the reservation were more open to bargaining for the Black Hills. But the chiefs could not agree with the government on the amount the Black Hills were worth. Neither side would budge. This made the commissioners angry. They returned to Washington, D.C. Their mission was a failure. Publicly, they told Congress that it should arrange one way or another to pay the Sioux the fair equivalent of what this land was worth. Privately, they and other officials determined that if the government could not buy their way into the Black Hills, they should simply arrange to take the land.

In November 1875, President Ulysses S. Grant faced a serious dilemma. Legally and morally, the Black Hills belonged to the Teton Sioux. But the public was eager to have the hills opened to white settlement. Already, thousands of miners had swarmed to the hills and staked their claims. The army had not really attempted to keep them out. Grant was determined to steal the Black Hills. This meant fighting the bands of Hunkpapas, northern Cheyenne, and other bands who considered it theirs. Now was the time to force Sitting Bull and the others to abandon the territory once and for all. If they refused to comply, the government was prepared to whip them into agreement. War, it seemed, was the only solution. But to make this attitude seem less brutal, Grant decided to give the bands one last chance. The government sent a message to the hunting bands in late December 1875. It said the Sioux must move to the reservation by January 31, 1876. If they failed to do so, they would be treated as "hostiles." Government troops would deal with them by force.

❖The Bands Scatter❖

In December 1875, Sitting Bull and the other hunting bands were widely scattered in small camps along the Powder River and its branches to the northeast of the Bighorn Mountains. It is unclear if government messengers got through to many of the camps with this important order. Deep snows, blinding blizzards, and dangerous wilderness trails made travel difficult. Reportedly, those bands that received the order responded in a calm manner. Deadlines were not in the Native American way of thinking. They simply saw the order as an invitation that they could not quite accept at the moment. Their response was something to the effect that when they were done hunting buffalo in the spring, it if were convenient, they would be happy to come talk. But, in the meantime, they had other things to do. To the various Teton Sioux and northern Cheyenne tribes, who went by a natural lunar calendar, the idea of doing anything according to the western calendar was a strange concept. Winter conditions also made it impossible for an entire camp to travel far. Word may have reached Sitting Bull, but it appears he had little idea of the approaching hostilities. He was living according to the old ways the entire winter of 1875–76.

❖The Army Goes into Action❖

On February 1, 1876, the day after the deadline was up, none of the hunting bands in the unceded territory had shown up at the reservation. So, the army went into action. The plan was for three columns of soldiers to converge on the Native American winter camps. The War Department would use its troops to bring the Native Americans to their knees. According to the War Department, the Native

Americans could not defend themselves against such a massive force of guns and firepower.

But the government had failed to take into account the toughness of its opponents. Sitting Bull had maintained strong ties with white traders in his territory. From them, he had kept his men well supplied with ammunition and rifles. The Teton Sioux and Cheyenne tribes had become closer over the last few years. They were drawn together during the various clashes with whites, whom they saw as a common enemy. Most importantly, they felt their cause was holy. They had confidence and faith in what they were fighting for. Their hand in battle would be strengthened by eternal spirits who would never fail them. They would be lead to victory.

As it turned out, bad weather prevented the army from carrying out its plan until early that spring. By mid-March, only one group, under General George Crook, had managed to get to an encampment of Native Americans on the Powder River. Crook's soldiers charged in and burned the village and drove away hundreds of horses. But it was hardly a great victory. Those Cheyenne and Teton Sioux tribes that survived this assault, known as the Battle of Powder River, managed to reclaim some of their horses. Then they straggled north and west several days in temperatures of minus 40 degrees, without food or rest. Eventually they reached Sitting Bull's camp at the mouth of the Tongue River. Sitting Bull immediately fed, clothed, and housed the exhausted and starving group of some three hundred people. Those who were among this tattered group never forgot the Hunkpapa chief's kindness to them on that day.

◈Fighting Together◈

The chiefs in the group met to decide what to do next. There was little debate. They all agreed. They must stay together and fight. All looked to Sitting Bull to lead them in their offensive. Word spread among the hunting bands of the threat from the soldiers. More and more bands started streaming toward Sitting Bull's camp. Northern Cheyennes, MiniConjous, Oglalas, and various other Teton Sioux tribes swelled the camp to more than four thousand. Of these, about one thousand were warriors.[2] This vast encampment used up so much firewood, small game, and grazing land that they had to move every few days. By late spring, they had made their way to Rosebud Creek in southeastern Montana.

◈Another Sun Dance◈

In June, which the natives called the Moon of Making Fat, Sitting Bull and his warriors made preparations for their annual Sun Dance. This year, the ritual had a special meaning. Sitting Bull and his people were facing a serious threat. He had prayed a few weeks before for *Wakantanka* to save him and his people. In return, he would participate in the Sun Dance. He would offer up a scarlet blanket of his blood to *Wakantanka*.

Before participating in the dance, Sitting Bull went, as usual, to the sweat lodge. Afterward, he was led to the Sun Dance lodge. There, he was rubbed all over with sage and his body painted with sacred symbols. His hands and feet were colored red. This was the hue of everything closest to *Wakantanka*. His shoulders were covered with blue stripes, representing the sky. After participating in a sacred pipe ceremony, Sitting Bull was ready.

He approached the dance circle and sat down. His adopted younger brother, Jumping Bull, made small cuts in Sitting Bull's arms in one hundred places. The chief was soon covered with blood. He never once cried. Instead he chanted prayers during the half-hour-long ordeal. Sacrifice of flesh like this would bring him closer to *Wakantanka*. This was the sacrifice he had promised to make.

Musicians began to blow on their shrill bone whistles and to beat their drums. Sitting Bull and the other Hunkpapa warriors in the dance were brought forward. Rawhide thongs and skewers were inserted into their chest. They danced until they pulled themselves free of the thongs. They leaned back, then, and started to move. All the while they stared at the sun and prayed. At night, they kept dancing. They prayed all the time to *Wakantanka* to come and speak to

— ◈ —

One of Sitting Bull's favorite children was Crow Foot. He was born about the time of the battle at the Little Bighorn. Crow Foot was killed, along with his father, at the time of Sitting Bull's arrest in 1890.

them. After several days, Sitting Bull slumped forward. He had pulled himself free. He was weak and in pain. But suddenly, he heard a voice. A vision came to him. He saw hundreds of blue-coated soldiers falling upside down, headfirst into a Native American village. They were tumbling like grasshoppers out of the sky. Their hats were flying off their heads. In the midst of the vision, Sitting Bull fainted. When he awoke, he knew immediately the meaning of what he had seen. He told everyone. The soldiers were coming toward them, to be killed. The Native Americans would be victorious. People cheered. Sitting Bull's vision gave those in the huge camp a new sense of confidence and faith in their purpose. Soon, the truth of Sitting Bull's prophecy would be put to the test.

Battle of the Rosebud and the Little Bighorn

Not long after the Sun Dance, in June of 1876, a small group of Cheyenne warriors from Sitting Bull's camp were out hunting. They spotted a group of soldiers heading in their direction. The bluecoats were part of General George Crook's troops. They had been sent to end the Plains tribes' resistance once and for all. There were three other columns of soldiers also heading toward a final showdown in "Indian country." Among them were forces under Colonel John Gibbon, of the military district of Montana, and the troops of General Alfred Terry. Terry was the commanding general of the Department of the Dakota. Serving under Terry was the 7th Cavalry, commanded by Lieutenant Colonel George "Long Hair" Custer. The army's plan was to trap Sitting Bull and the Sioux, Cheyenne, and Arapaho forces that had joined him. They aimed to converge on the warriors from several directions at once. The three columns of troops would perform a pincer movement. They would close in on their target like the claws of a crab, making escape all but impossible.

❖Custer Moves In❖

The Cheyenne raced back to Sitting Bull to warn him and the others of impending danger. Immediately the tribes picked up camp and moved west. A band of scouts led by the Cheyenne warrior Little Hawk stayed behind. They would keep track of the soldiers' movements. By that night, June 16, General Crook neared Sitting Bull's recent campsite on the Rosebud. Little Hawk's scouts rode off to keep Sitting Bull informed. Sitting Bull told his chiefs to leave the soldiers alone unless they attacked first. But, in the middle of the night, a familiar pattern was repeated: Some impatient young warriors from Sitting Bull's camp rode out, eager to attack the enemy. Sitting Bull and Crazy Horse had little choice but to follow behind as a back-up force.

Early the next morning, June 17, Crook's scouts told him of approaching hostile bands. He was not

— ❖ —

Sitting Bull waged many battles with United States' troops in his attempt to maintain freedom for Native Americans.

worried. The Sioux and Cheyenne had so far shown no willingness to fight. So, the General and his men sat around the camp, playing cards and drinking coffee. They heard some distant shots and commented that their scouts must be hunting buffalo again. Before long, it was apparent what the gunfire was really about. Crook's Crow scouts charged into camp screaming that the Sioux were approaching. The soldiers barely had time to prepare for a battle when the Sioux and Cheyenne appeared. They launched one attack after another.

❖Attacks Are Launched❖

One of Crook's men, Captain Anson Mills, described the attackers as a fierce-looking band covered with war paint and wearing nothing but moccasins, breechcloths, and feathered headdresses. He later judged the several hundred mounted warriors that came at him that day as among the best cavalry he had ever seen. The attackers had perfected their technique. As they approached the soldiers, they would suddenly drop down to one side of their horses. They clung to their horses with one arm and a leg, while flinging their lances from under the horses' necks. In this way, the warriors were protected from the soldiers' aim, yet could skillfully launch their own attacks.

Fighting went on all morning and into the afternoon. The men charged back and forth at each other.

The superior firepower of the soldiers kept the Native Americans at bay. Finally, as evening approached, the Sioux and Cheyenne forces called off the fight and headed back to camp. Crook claimed victory at this Battle of the Rosebud. But the actual victory belonged, in fact, to the Sioux and Cheyenne. They had battled a force double their own size and kept it off balance with fierce, repeated thrusts.

❖Victory in Battle❖

They traveled most of the previous night and fought all day. They were exhausted, but had fought a hard battle. The following morning, they moved farther south and west to camp in the valley of the Little Bighorn River. The Teton Sioux called this the Greasy Grass River. This area is located in southeastern Montana Territory, and was still a vast wilderness. Thickets of cottonwood trees and underbrush lined the river that flowed from the snow-capped mountains to the east. From the edge of the mountains, the lush valley stretched out to a rim of gentle, grassy hills. It was here, in the midst of this peaceful landscape, that the Sioux now arranged their circles of tipis, band-by-band. By the time the camp was set up, tipis stretched for several miles across the valley floor. Sitting Bull and his band camped in a watchful, protective position at the southern edge of the camp.

As soon as they had set up their lodges that evening, the Cheyenne and Sioux warriors danced and feasted in celebration of their recent victory. The next day, the children splashed and played in the river. The women poked about the river bottom, picking berries and digging wild roots. Some of the men tended to the horses. Others, who had been dancing until dawn, slept in their tipis. Joining this loose-knit camp were some warriors from the Great Sioux Reservation. Many still resented the white invasion of their Black Hills. They left the confines of the reservation to hunt with their brothers. They came, too, to band together for a last stand to save what was left of their land. Each day, more and more people trickled into the camp, swelling its size. By week's end, seven thousand Native Americans, including nearly two thousand fighting warriors, were gathered here. Never before had so many Plains warriors united together in one spot.[1]

❖The Little Bighorn❖

Meanwhile, General Terry planned his next move. He had heard of the encampment of hostile tribes near the Little Bighorn. His scouts told him that it included only about eight hundred warriors.[2] He figured that Custer's men would easily overpower this force. The plan was for Custer to move in and smash the camp from the east. Meanwhile Terry and Gibbon would be stationed just to the north of the camp to stop any fugitives fleeing in that direction. Custer was instructed to await the arrival of those northern reinforcements before attacking. But those who knew "Long Hair" figured he would ignore that command and try to attack on his own. He would be eager to win all the glory for himself.

Indeed, Custer moved toward the Little Bighorn Valley. The sun rose slowly over the mountains on the morning of June 25, 1876. Just at that moment, Custer's scouts rode up to the top of a hill known as the Crow's Nest. In the distance, they caught sight of a herd of horses. (They could not see the enemy encampment, but they assumed it must be nearby.) They were unaware of the size of the force they were about to encounter. Custer decided to press ahead. He split his force up, sending some to the southwest, while others, under Major Marcus Reno, were to attack the camp from the south. Still a third group under Custer himself was to head northward. They would block the Native Americans who tried to flee once attacked.

At the sound of the first shots, Sitting Bull grabbed his mother and his sister. Together, the three of them headed out of camp. Once out of danger he dropped them off, then returned to camp. As the tribal elder, Sitting Bull's role was defined by custom. He was not to prepare for battle. His job was to stay close to camp, where he could protect the women and chil-dren and offer up prayers for his people. Knowing this, the great chief kept some weapons. He gave his shield and bow and arrows to One Bull, who was his adopted son and nephew. Amid the dust and confusion of the attack, Sitting Bull mounted his horse and rode throughout camp, shouting words of encouragement to his warriors.

As the warriors headed out to meet the attack, they were led by Gall. The first round of bullets had killed his two wives and three children. He flew into the attack, armed with nothing but his hatchet. From the start, Reno's force of over one hundred men were no match for their opponents. Warriors darted swiftly in and around the soldiers, with wild whoops and weapons raised. The soldiers drew back to some timber near the river to form a defensive line. But the line was soon smashed by the warriors' lightninglike attacks. Reno pulled his men back to the nearest river crossing. The warriors gave chase, with Crazy Horse in the lead. The soldiers desperately tried to spur their mounts down the steep riverbank and across the stream to safety. Many fell in the turbulent water and perished. Altogether, Reno lost more than thirty men and nearly as many were wounded or unaccounted for.

Custer had made his way north of the camp. He was unaware of the slaughter of Reno's troops. He still believed the opposition would try to flee rather than fight. When the warriors realized that Custer's troops posed yet another challenge to the north, they momentarily froze with fear. But Sitting Bull rode up to his men at that point and told them not to give up.

He urged them to be like the bird who sees its enemy and then covers its nest and eggs to protect the young. All of Sitting Bull's warriors found renewed courage and raced out to fight on behalf of their families. Then, they regrouped for yet another battle. Sitting Bull rode along with them, reminding them to be brave. He stayed nearby, as the warriors waded across the Little Bighorn and headed north up the hillside toward Custer's assembled troops.

❖Custer Surprised❖

Custer was met by a fierce fighting force three times the size of his own. Many warriors got off their horses and advanced on foot through the underbrush. They came close to the soldiers and fired both arrows and bullets from repeating rifles. Custer's men tried to form a line to ward off the attacking force. Crazy Horse, however, led a charge to the rear of the line. Custer's soldiers were now surrounded on all sides. They ran like rabbits, most falling prey to their attackers. The sound of gunfire, warrior whoops, and eagle-bone war whistles filled the air. Dense clouds of dust swirled around the men. When the battlefield cleared, "Long Hair" and all of his men were dead or dying. As for the tribes, they had suffered, too. Thirty braves had died and dozens more had been wounded. Some fighting continued during the day against Reno's forces. The warriors could not shake them. Finally, when it seemed as though the battle would

— ❖ —

This painting by Richard Lorentz, called "Last Glow of a Passing Nation," depicts the Native American victory on June 25, 1876, at the Little Bighorn. As one Sioux warrior who partook of the battle put it, "Custer's troops were overwhelmed by the charging Indians like a hurricane . . . like bees swarming out of a hive."

continue indefinitely, Sitting Bull and his men withdrew.

Sitting Bull's men packed their things and gathered their horses and weapons. Following Sitting Bull's advice, they slowly headed south. To cover their trail and prevent the soldiers from coming after them, they set fire to the prairie grass along the riverbed as they went. A giant cloud of smoke hid their departure from view and allowed them to make their escape.

In the protective position to the rear rode Sitting Bull. His vision had been true. Soldiers had attacked their peaceful village. Yet despite the Native Americans' victory, Sitting Bull had seen too much killing to rejoice. Still, he felt proud. His wise leadership had brought together the spectacular gathering of tribes that had won at the Battle of the Little Bighorn. But this was to be their first and last great victory. Whether Sitting Bull knew it or not, this stunning success by the united tribes had spelled their certain doom.

FLIGHT, SURRENDER, DEATH

After the Battle of the Little Bighorn, the United States government and the army sought revenge for Custer's death. They would use any and all means to force the hunting bands to surrender. The American people were outraged by the death of their hero, Custer. They seemed unaware of the fact that the battle had been started by the soldiers' attack on a peaceful Native American village. Most were equally ignorant of the government's non-compliance with the Fort Laramie Treaty. The war against the tribes had been launched as an excuse to take over the Black Hills. The treaty had guaranteed this land to the Native Americans. War was the government's method of grabbing the Black Hills and the remaining hunting grounds from those very same tribes.

❖Unaware of Danger❖

After the Little Bighorn, Sitting Bull and his allied chiefs for a time failed to realize the danger they faced. They could not read the news reports. They were not aware of the public outcry against them. Hunting and gathering food remained their main concerns. They agreed to split up the huge camp of hunting bands. It was difficult finding enough food and grazing land for so large a group. Smaller bands could more easily follow the buffalo and not use up all the food in an area.

❖Search Continues❖

Meanwhile, the white soldiers continued their search for the tribes. At dawn on September 9, 1876, the battle lines were drawn again. Troops under General Crook's command stumbled upon an encampment of Hunkpapas, including Sitting Bull, located north of the Black Hills. They attacked. Sitting Bull, wearing a magnificent feathered headdress, rose to the fight. He raced to a high bluff, overlooking the site and got off a series of rounds at the soldiers. However, he and his people were greatly outnumbered and suffered a defeat. Many women and children were killed at this battle.

In the months that followed, battles between groups of natives and white soldiers intensified. In October, troops under Colonel Nelson A. Miles were setting in for the winter at the mouth of the Tongue River. They got a note:

> *I want to know what you are doing traveling on this road. You scare all the buffalo away. I want to hunt. . . . I want you to turn back from here. If you don't, I will fight you again.*

It was signed

> *I am your friend, Sitting Bull.[1]*

Later that same month, Sitting Bull and Colonel Miles, whom the Sioux called "Bear Coat" because of his fur-collared coat, met a few times. Sitting Bull wanted to know why the soldiers were still in his territory. He told Miles he would not fire on the soldiers if they left the area. Sitting Bull refused to surrender. He told Miles that he preferred to live without annuities or government rations and to be left to "live as an Indian."[2] But hostilities continued between the two sides. In December, Miles captured and burned Sitting Bull's camp at Redwater Creek in eastern Montana. A month later, Miles again attacked Sitting Bull, forcing him and his people to flee. All winter long, the soldiers bothered the Teton Sioux and Northern Cheyenne. The hunting tribes and their leaders, including Crazy Horse, were exhausted from the constant strain of being under attack or on the run. During the next few months, many of the Native Americans streamed into reservations to surrender to government authorities.

❖Escape to Canada❖

In early May 1877, Sitting Bull and about one thousand of his people sought relief from attack in a different way. They fled across the border into Canada. Here, they joined a group of their people who had already been there for several months. Sitting Bull established a camp about sixty miles north of the Montana border in what would become the province of Saskatchewan. Major James M. Walsh of the Northwest Mounted Police rode fearlessly into Sitting Bull's camp and told him the rules he expected the Native Americans to follow. They were not allowed to cross back into the United States to hunt, steal, or fight. If they violated these terms, they would not be permitted to stay in Canada. In return the Canadians agreed to protect Sitting Bull and his people from attacks by American soldiers, should the troops cross the border and come after them. Sitting Bull was satisfied with these terms. Under the circumstances, he had no wish to return to his homeland. In truth, the United States did not want Sitting Bull back either. The United States now had the Sioux problem out of their hands. In fact, United States officials pressed Canada to formally accept these people and offer them food and shelter. However, the Canadians had their own tribes to deal with and did not want the official responsibility of the Sioux, too. Sitting Bull and his people continued to strain relations between the United States and Canada. As time went on, Canadian officials began pressing Sitting Bull to return to the United States.

❖Life in Canada❖

Life in Canada was becoming tougher for Sitting Bull and his people. Buffalo were scarce, and many in his camp were hungry. Shots were often fired at those Sioux who, in defiance of their agreement with the Canadians, crossed the border into Montana to hunt. More and more of Sitting Bull's people deserted him and went south to live on reservations in the United States. Finally, there were only several hundred left. Most of them were old men, women, and children. As conditions worsened, Sitting Bull faced a dilemma. Should he stay with his people on the brink of famine, or surrender? At least on a reservation, they would all be fed. Finally, for the sake of the starving children, Sitting Bull chose the latter. On July 19, 1881, he crossed back into the United States and arrived in Fort Buford. He was wearing a soiled shirt and black leggings, with a worn-out blanket draped about his waist. "Let it be recorded," he said, "that I am the last of my people to lay down my gun."[3] After surrendering his weapon, Sitting Bull and two hundred of his frightened followers were escorted via steamer down the Missouri River to the Standing Rock Agency at Fort Yates. Sitting Bull had been promised his own place to live. He was told he could rejoin his people in his old homeland. But in September, the government went back on its promises. Sitting Bull might cause trouble at Standing Rock. So, the defeated chief was moved farther down the Missouri River to Fort Randall. Here, he was held under close watch for nearly two years as a military prisoner.

❖National Celebrity❖

In the spring of 1883, Sitting Bull and more than one hundred fifty followers who had been held at Fort Randall were allowed to return to Standing Rock. They were resigned to making a new life for themselves. Soon, Sitting Bull became quite a national celebrity. Numerous articles about him appeared in the press and he was allowed to travel a bit outside the reservation.

❖Teams With Buffalo Bill❖

In 1885, he took the unlikely step of joining William F. "Buffalo Bill" Cody's popular Wild West Show. Dressed in full costume, Sitting Bull was introduced to audiences with great fanfare. He performed throughout the country. Most everyone loved him and greeted his appearance with applause. This warrior

— ✦ —

This drawing from Harper's Weekly *depicts the formal surrender that took place on July 19, 1881, when Sitting Bull and his followers streamed toward Fort Buford from their exile in Canada.*

had spent his past life fighting the white men and their way of life. Now he was paraded about as a showman in their midst. Actually, Sitting Bull had several good reasons for joining Buffalo Bill's show. First, it gave him some freedom: The group toured more than a dozen cities in the United States and in Canada. He also earned fifty dollars a week. Most of this money he gave away to the needy—especially ragged little white boys he saw in the cities. Sitting Bull, like many of his people, considered it unthinkable to keep money or food from those less fortunate. In addition, Buffalo Bill treated him and the other Native Americans in the show with respect. However, when the season ended in the fall of that year, Sitting Bull decided to quit. There was talk of the government

— ❖ —

Sitting Bull (left) is shown here with William F. "Buffalo Bill" Cody. Sitting Bull joined Cody's Wild West Show in 1885.

seizing more Sioux lands. He felt he was needed by his people. At the end of his time with the show, he received two gifts from Buffalo Bill: a large white cowboy hat and Cody's circus horse. It had been trained to stand on its hind legs and lift one front hoof at the sound of gunfire. Sitting Bull treasured these presents until the day he died.

Indeed, Sitting Bull was needed by his people. The government planned to divide their reservation up into six smaller ones. This would end up depriving the Native Americans of land. It would also open up more of the reservation to eager settlers. The government promised the Sioux that it would pay them for the territory they had to give up. Sitting Bull and others resisted. But after fighting the settlement for a year, most of the tribes finally consented in 1889 to move to smaller reservations. Sitting Bull was not invited to the final meeting where the agreement was made. When he heard of what had happened, he was furious and shouted, "There are no Indians left but me!"[4] Further, he claimed the Sioux Nation was now "a thing of the past," because "Without land, we are nothing."[5]

Sitting Bull's resistance to the white man kept his high status among his people on the reservation. But he was helpless to do anything about many of their troubles. Drought, crop failures, and various "white" diseases, such as measles, pneumonia, and tuberculosis, all took their toll on the reservation Sioux. To make things worse, the government cut the reservation's beef rations in half. The Sioux also never received the money promised for their land.

❖A New Religion❖

In the midst of these difficulties, rumors of a new religion from farther west began swirling about the reservation. In 1890 a Sioux named Kicking Bear brought word to the Standing Rock Reservation of the Ghost Dance. The dance originated in Nevada as part of a new religion conceived by a Paiute holy man, named Wovoka. It seemed to combine elements of Christianity and Native American beliefs. Kicking Bear's account excited the suffering Sioux at the Standing Rock Reservation. According to Wovoka, if the Native Americans adopted this new faith and performed the Ghost Dance, they could live forever in a land without white people, sickness, or hunger. It promised a vision of heaven on earth, a future in which all land would be inhabited by Native Americans. There would be abundant game, and everything else they needed. To make this happen, everybody should dance. They should not be afraid of the whites. Wovoka promised that if they wore a special ghost shirt, it would keep them from all harm, including bullets. The Ghost Dance religion soon gripped Standing Rock. The government-appointed agent there, Major James McLaughlin, did all he could to stop it, but to no avail. The bands formed a ring of tipis as a dance circle north of Sitting Bull's cluster of

— ❖ —

James B. McLaughlin, shown here, was the agent at the Standing Rock Reservation who ordered Sitting Bull's arrest. He had battled with Sitting Bull for seven years before this.

cabins. Each morning they would purify themselves in the sweat lodge, then begin to dance and continue dancing all day. McLaughlin and other officials feared that the dancing would cause unrest and rebellion. Throughout the winter, Sitting Bull presided over the group of dancers and made no move to stop them. Officials came up with a list of troublemakers involved with the Ghost Dance. Sitting Bull's name was on the list.

❖Police Arrive❖

At 6 A.M. on December 15, 1890, forty-three Sioux policemen, employed by the United States government, arrived at Sitting Bull's cabin. They were there to arrest him. They forced him out of bed and told him he must come with them. Initially, he agreed. Nonetheless, the policemen started pushing and shoving him. Sitting Bull braced himself against the door and cried out, "Let me go. I'll go without any assistance."[6] Word of the arrest spread quickly throughout the reservation. Soon a crowd had gathered around Sitting Bull's cabin. People were screaming at the police not to take their chief. As he stumbled outside and realized the number of people gathered there defending him, Sitting Bull had a sudden change of heart. He began to put up a fight and to resist arrest. Just then, one of the crowd fired a shot at the arresting policeman named Bull Head. Bull Head fell. As he went down, he aimed and hit

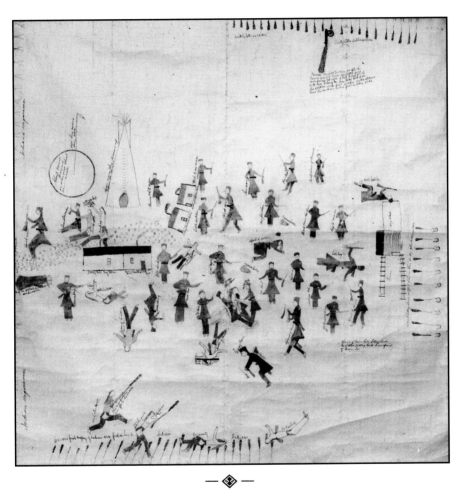

— ❖ —

This pictograph, presumably painted by a Sioux, shows the arrest and death of Sitting Bull.

Sitting Bull in the chest. At the same time, another policeman, Red Tomahawk, fired and the shot hit Sitting Bull in the back of the head. The Hunkpapa chief crumbled and died immediately. As the shots rang out, Sitting Bull's circus horse did as he had been trained: he reared up and held out his hoof. Ferocious fighting continued around Sitting Bull's body. In the end, seven members of his band, including his beloved son, Crow Foot, and six policemen lay dead.[7]

❖Proud to the End❖

Sitting Bull had kept his pride to the end. His last stance, like his life, was one of proud resistance. He went down with his fighting spirit intact. Equally and eerily intact were his powers of prophecy. One morning not too long before his death, Sitting Bull had gone for a walk out on the reservation grounds. Suddenly he had heard a voice. He stopped and looked around and saw a meadowlark. He had long had a special relationship with the meadowlarks. He could communicate with them. He listened as this bird told him that he would soon die at the hands of his own people. Returning from his walk, he was somber. He never forgot that moment. In the end, death did not take him by surprise.

❖Wounded Knee❖

After Sitting Bull's death, a group of three hundred fifty Sioux, many of them Ghost Dancers, under a leader named Chief Big Foot, fled into the Badlands.

Custer's old unit, the 7th Cavalry followed them. On December 28, 1890, the Sioux surrendered. The next morning, the soldiers surrounded the Sioux at their camp on Wounded Knee Creek and demanded their weapons. When one Sioux resisted, his gun went off accidentally. Immediately, gunshots rang out on all sides, and many natives fled in fear. In the end, some two hundred Sioux, mostly all women and children, lay dead in the deep snow.[8] For years afterward, this massacre at Wounded Knee, as the Sioux called it, poisoned relations between the Sioux and whites. It still does to this day.

◈Sitting Bull's Legacy◈

Sitting Bull remained true to his principles all his life. He left a proud legacy. He commanded great respect from his people because of his devotion to their old values and ways. He was deeply in touch with nature and the spiritual world. Sitting Bull became a respected holy man. He was a visionary among his people. As a chief, he stood for bravery and courage, generosity and wisdom—all the virtues that the Hunkpapas most valued. Though he was ultimately defeated and forced into the reservation way of life, he never fully gave in. While others made deals with the reservation authorities, as a way of buying favors or making their lives easier, Sitting Bull refused to do so. He chose instead to fight many small battles on behalf of his people. Today, more than one hundred years after his death, his name still commands respect.

CHRONOLOGY

1831 ❖ Baby Slow is born in present-day South Dakota.

1841 ❖ Slow participates in his first hunt and kills his first buffalo.

1845 ❖ Slow has his first success in battle. He counts his first coup and is given the name Sitting Bull.

1850 ❖ Sitting Bull achieves the rank of warrior/hunter.

1856 ❖ Sitting Bull receives a wound in his foot.

1857 ❖ Sitting Bull becomes a war chief and adopts an Assiniboine named Stays Back as his brother.

1863 ❖ Sitting Bull joins the fight with the Dakota Sioux, against forces led by Henry H. Sibley.

1864 ❖ Sitting Bull takes part in the Battle of Killdeer Mountain.

1868 ❖ Sitting Bull hosts Father Pierre-Jean De Smet prior to the signing of the Fort Laramie Treaty.

Late 1860s ❖ Sitting Bull is elevated to the rank of chief during the June Sun Dance.

1876 ❖ Sitting Bull participates in the Sun Dance, and relates his vision of soldiers falling upside down. He serves as respected elder during the Battle of the Little Bighorn, a victory over Army forces. He participates in the Battle of Slim Buttes.

1881 ❖ Sitting Bull surrenders to United States authorities at Fort Buford and is sent to Fort Randall as a military prisoner.

1883 ❖ Sitting Bull is allowed to settle at Standing Rock.

1885 ❖ Sitting Bull travels with "Buffalo Bill" Cody's Wild West Show.

1890 ❖ Sitting Bull is killed.

CHAPTER NOTES

Chapter 1

1. Robert M. Utley, *The Lance and the Shield: The Life and Times of Sitting Bull* (New York: Henry Holt & Company, 1993), p. 53.

2. Ibid., p. 34.

Chapter 2

1. All names are taken from Robert M. Utley, *The Lance and the Shield: The Life and Times of Sitting Bull* (New York: Henry Holt & Company, 1993).

2. Russell Freedman, *Buffalo Hunt* (New York: Holiday House, 1988), p. 50.

Chapter 3

1. Stanley Vestal, *Sitting Bull: Champion of the Sioux* (Norman, Okla.: University of Oklahoma Press, 1957), p. 9.

2. Richard O'Connor, *Sitting Bull: War Chief of the Sioux* (New York: McGraw-Hill, 1968), p. 13.

3. Vestal, p.12.

Chapter 4

1. Robert M. Utley, *The Lance and the Shield: The Life and Times of Sitting Bull* (New York: Henry Holt & Company, 1993), p. 30.

2. Ibid.

3. Lisa Eisenberg, *The Story of Sitting Bull, Great Sioux Chief* (New York: Dell, 1991), p. 35.

Chapter 5

1. Sheila Black, *Sitting Bull and the Battle of the Little Bighorn* (Englewood Cliffs, N.J.: Silver Burdett Press, 1989), p. 31.

2. Ibid., p. 32.

3. Richard O'Connor, *Sitting Bull: War Chief of the Sioux* (New York: McGraw-Hill, 1968), p. 42.

4. Robert M. Utley, *The Lance and the Shield: The Life and Times of Sitting Bull* (New York: Henry Holt & Company, 1993), p. 63.

5. Russell Freedman, *Indian Chiefs* (New York: Holiday House, 1987), p. 119.

6. Lisa Eisenberg, *The Story of Sitting Bull, Great Sioux Chief* (New York: Dell, 1991), p. 50.

Chapter 6

1. Sheila Black, *Sitting Bull and the Battle of the Little Bighorn* (Englewood Cliffs, N.J.: Silver Burdett Press, 1989), p. 68.

2. Lisa Eisenberg, *The Story of Sitting Bull, Great Sioux Chief* (New York: Dell, 1991), p. 53.

3. Russell Freedman, *Indian Chiefs*, (New York: Holiday House, 1987), p. 118.

4. Editors of Time-Life Books, *The War for the Plains* (Alexandria, Va.: Time-Life Books, 1994), p. 141.

5. Clarence L. Ver Steeg and Richard Hofstadter, *A People and a Nation* (New York: Harper & Row, 1971), p. 382.

6. Ibid., p. 376.

7. Black, p. 52.

Chapter 7

1. Sheila Black, *Sitting Bull and the Battle of the Little Bighorn* (Englewood Cliffs, N.J.: Silver Burdett Press, 1989), p. 78.

2. Editors of Time-Life Books, *The War for the Plains* (Alexandria, Va.: Time-Life Books, 1994), p. 145.

Chapter 8

1. Editors of Time-Life Books, *The War for the Plains* (Alexandria, Va.: Time-Life Books, 1994), p. 150.

2. Ibid., p. 152.

Chapter 9

1. Joseph Manzione, *"I Am Looking to the North For My Life": Sitting Bull, 1876–1881* (Salt Lake City, Utah: University of Utah Press, 1991), p. 23.

2. Ibid., p. 25.

3. Richard O'Connor, *Sitting Bull: War Chief of the Sioux* (New York: McGraw-Hill, 1968), p. 110.

4. Lisa Eisenberg, *The Story of Sitting Bull, Great Sioux Chief* (New York: Dell, 1991), p. 98.

5. O'Connor, p. 122.

6. Robert M. Utley, *The Lance and the Shield: The Life and Times of Sitting Bull* (New York: Henry Holt & Company, 1993), p. 300.

7. Ibid.

8. Ibid., p. 302.

☞ GLOSSARY ☜

❖ **badlands**—Rugged, fantastically formed hills.

❖ **bluff**—A hill.

❖ **bridle**—The headgear with which a horse is controlled.

❖ **butte**—Steep-sided, towering rocks.

❖ **cavalry**—Troops mounted on horseback.

❖ **civilian**—A person not on active duty in a military, police, or firefighting force.

❖ **contempt**—A lack of respect.

❖ **cradleboard**—A wooden board on which a baby could be placed to travel.

❖ **ermine**—A small weasel.

❖ **geologist**—A scientist who studies the history of the earth and its life, especially as recorded in rocks.

❖ **hardtack**—Hard biscuits of flower and water.

❖ **pemmican**—A food prepared by mixing dried meat with fat and berries; it could be stored for long periods of time.

❖ **pincer movement**—Closing in on a target like the claws of a crab.

❖ **plateau**—A level stretch of raised land.

❖ **pronghorn**—An antelopelike animal the size of a large goat, with prongs on its horns.

❖ **reservation**—An area set aside by the government to be the permanent home of a group of Native Americans.

❖ **saddle horn**—A knob on the front of a saddle.

❖ **sorrel**—A light brown or chestnut-colored horse.

❖ **Sun Dance**—A ritual of Sioux warriors. The dance thanked the Great Spirit for past favors and insured a favorable future.

❖ **supplication**—Prayer.

❖ **treaties**—Agreements between two groups. Treaties between the United States and Native Americans often dealt with the sale of land.

FURTHER READING

Adler, David A. *A Picture Book of Sitting Bull*. New York: Holiday House, 1993.

Andrews, Elaine K. *Indians of the Plains*. New York: Facts on File, 1992.

Black, Sheila. *Sitting Bull and the Battle of the Little Bighorn*. Englewood Cliffs, N.J.: Silver Burdett Press, 1989.

Bleeker, Sonia. *The Sioux Indians: Hunters and Warriors of the Plains*. New York: William Morrow, 1962.

Capps, Benjamin, and the Editors of Time-Life Books. *The Great Chiefs*. Alexandria, Va.: Time-Life Books, 1975.

Editors of Time-Life Books. *The Buffalo Hunters*. Alexandria, Va.: Time-Life Books, 1993.

———. *The War for the Plains*. Alexandria, Va.: Time-Life Books, 1994.

Eisenberg, Lisa. *The Story of Sitting Bull, Great Sioux Chief*. New York: Dell, 1991.

Freedman, Russell. *Buffalo Hunt*. New York: Holiday House, 1988.

———. *Indian Chiefs*. New York: Holiday House, 1987.

Manzione, Joseph. *"I Am Looking to the North for My Life": Sitting Bull, 1876–1881*. Salt Lake City, Utah: University of Utah Press, 1991.

McGovern, Ann. *If You Lived with the Sioux Indians*. New York: Scholastic, Inc., 1972.

O'Connor, Richard. *Sitting Bull: War Chief of the Sioux*. New York: McGraw-Hill, 1968.

Sanford, William R. *Sitting Bull: Sioux Warrior*. Springfield, N.J.: Enslow Publishers, 1994.

Utley, Robert M. *The Lance and the Shield: The Life and Times of Sitting Bull*. New York: Henry Holt & Company, 1993.

Vestal, Stanley. *Sitting Bull: Champion of the Sioux*. Norman, Okla.: University of Oklahoma Press, 1957.

Wolfson, Evelyn. *The Teton Sioux: People of the Plains*. Brookfield, Conn.: Millbrook Press, 1992.

➣➤ INDEX ⫷⫸